Feeling Angry

by Helen Frost

Consulting Editor: Gail Saunders-Smith, Ph.D.

Consultant: Erik Willcutt, Ph.D.
Child Clinical Psychologist
Instructor, University of Denver

Pebble Books

an imprint of Capstone Press
Mankato, Minnesota

Pebble Books are published by Capstone Press
1710 Roe Crest Drive, North Mankato, Minnesota 56003
www.capstonepub.com

Books published by Capstone Press are manufactured with paper
containing at least 10 percent post-consumer waste.

Library of Congress Cataloging-in-Publication Data
Frost, Helen, 1949–
    Feeling angry / by Helen Frost.
        p. cm.—(Emotions)
    Includes bibliographical references and index.
    Summary: Simple text and photographs describe and illustrate anger and ways
to alleviate it.
        ISBN-13: 978-0-7368-0668-8 (hardcover)   ISBN-10: 0-7368-0668-7 (hardcover)
        ISBN-13: 978-0-7368-4843-5 (softcover)   ISBN-10: 0-7368-4843-6 (softcover)
    1. Anger in children—Juvenile literature. [1. Anger.] I. Title. II. Emotions
(Mankato, Minn.)
BF723.A4F76   2001
152.4′7—dc21   00-025021

Note to Parents and Teachers

The Emotions series supports national health education standards
related to interpersonal communication and expression of feelings.
This book describes and illustrates the feeling of anger. The
photographs support emergent readers in understanding the
text. The repetition of words and phrases helps emergent readers
learn new words. This book also introduces emergent readers to
subject-specific vocabulary words, which are defined in the Words
to Know section. Emergent readers may need assistance to read
some words and to use the Table of Contents, Words to Know, Read
More, Internet Sites, and Index/Word List sections of the book.

Printed in the United States of America in North Mankato, Minnesota.
102012   006929R

Table of Contents

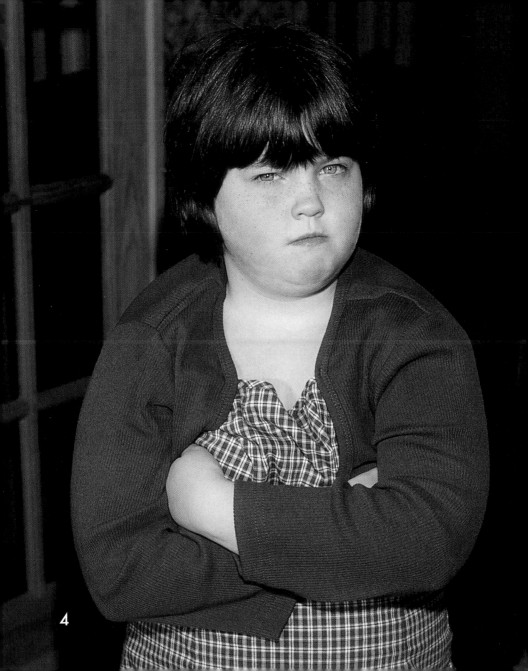

You feel mad
when you are angry.

Everyone feels
angry sometimes.

You might feel angry
when someone is mean.

You might feel angry
when something is not fair.

You might feel like yelling when you are angry.

You might feel like hitting
when you are angry.

You can learn
to control your anger.

You can talk about
what makes you angry.

You can try to change what makes you angry.

Words to Know

control—to hold back; people can express anger in ways that do not hurt others.

fair—reasonable and just; people can work to make situations fair.

yell—to shout, cry out, or scream loudly; yelling does not help anger to go away.

Read More

Althea. *Feeling Angry.* Exploring Emotions.
Milwaukee: Gareth Stevens Publishing, 1998.

Doudna, Kelly. *I Feel Angry. How Do You Feel?*
Minneapolis: Abdo & Daughters, 1999.

Johnson, Julie. *Being Angry.* How Do I Feel About.
Brookfield, Conn.: Copper Beech Books, 1999.

Johnston, Marianne. *Dealing with Anger.* The
Conflict Resolution Library. New York: PowerKids
Press, 1996.

Internet Sites

FactHound offers a safe, fun way to
find Internet sites related to this book.

Go to *www.facthound.com*

He'll fetch the best sites for you!

FactHound will fetch the best sites for you!

Index/Word List

Word Count: 70
Early-Intervention Level: 6

Editorial Credits
Mari C. Schuh, editor; Kia Bielke, designer; Katy Kudela, photo researcher

Photo Credits
David F. Clobes, 6, 18
Jack Glisson, 1
K. D. Dittlinger, 10
Kim Stanton, 8, 12, 14, 16
Matt Swinden, 20
Unicorn Stock Photos/B. W. Hoffmann, cover
Visuals Unlimited/Eric Anderson, 4

The author thanks the children's section staff at the Allen County Public Library in Fort Wayne, Indiana, for research assistance.

24